Gold! Hidden Stories of Australia's Past
Book 3

Gold and the Chinese:

Racism, Riots and Protest on the Australian Goldfields

Marji Hill

Published by The Prison Tree Press 2022

Copyright © 2022 Marji Hill
Copyright © 2022 Artwork and paintings by Marji Hill

Editor: Eddie Dowd

Cover image is a painting by Marji Hill and is based on the Bendigo Joss House Temple

ISBN 978-0-6454834-4-4 (paperback)
ISBN 978-0-6454834-5-1 (eBook)

The Prison Tree Press
Suite 124, 1-10 Albert Avenue
Broadbeach, Queensland 4218

https://marjihill.com
https://www.fastselfpublishing.com

 A catalogue record for this work is available from the National Library of Australia

All rights reserved. No part of this book may be reproduced, stored in a retrieval system, or transmitted in any form or by any means, electronic, mechanical, photocopying, recording, scanning, or otherwise, without the prior written permission of the publisher.

Disclaimer
All the material contained in this book is provided for educational and informational purposes only. No responsibility can be taken for any results or outcomes resulting from the use of this material.

While every care has been taken to trace and acknowledge copyright the publishers tender their apologies for any accidental infringement where copyright has proved untraceable.

Every attempt has been made to provide information that is both accurate and effective, however, the author does not assume any responsibility for the accuracy or use/misuse of this information.

Gold and the Chinese is the story of the Chinese on the Australian goldfields: the abuse, misunderstanding and discrimination against them and how these anti-Chinese sentiments led to institutionalised racism.

READ about the Asian visitors to Australia who were part of a great north-south trade route stretching from China to Australia and back.

LEARN about the arrival of the Chinese, who contributed greatly to the Australian story, but whose migration to the goldfields gave birth to racist, anti-Chinese sentiment.

FIND OUT why there was this ill-feeling towards the Chinese.

DISCOVER how the White Australia Policy was shaped by decades of anti-Chinese sentiment extending back to the goldfields.

READ about the stories of violence against the Chinese in Victoria's Buckland Valley and at Lambing Flat in New South Wales.

and much more...

THE SERIES
Gold! Hidden Stories of Australia's Past

Book 1
The Gates of Gold:
The Discovery of Gold, its Legacy and Australian Identity

Book 2
Shadows of Gold:
Eureka and the Birth of Australian democracy

Book 3
Gold and the Chinese:
Racism, Riots and Protest on the Australian Goldfields

Book 4
Ghosts of Gold:
The Life and Times of Jupiter Mosman

Book 5
Blood Gold:
Native Police, Bushrangers & Lawlessness on the Australian Goldfields

Dedication

To the memory
of those of Chinese heritage
who came to Australia,
of those who stayed
and those who returned to China

TABLE OF CONTENTS

Chapter 1 — Early Visitors	1
Chapter 2 — Early Chinese Migrants	19
Chapter 3 — Discovery of gold	25
Chapter 4 — Anti-Chinese Legislation	35
Chapter 5 — Buckland Valley	53
Chapter 6 — Lambing Flat	63
Chapter 7 — Expanding Frontiers	81
Sources	103
Questions for further Consideration	109
About Marji Hill	111
More Books by Marji Hill	117

ACKNOWLEDGEMENTS

I acknowledge the Traditional Custodians of Country throughout Australia and their connections to land, sea, and community. I pay my respect to elders, past, present, and emerging and extend my respect to all First Nations peoples today.

In the spirit of reconciliation, my mission is to increase understanding between the First Nations and other Australians and to provide people from all over the globe some basic understanding of Australia's first people, their history, and cultures.

In my life I've been fortunate to have had several mentors. Alex Barlow, my late partner, would always say to me "If you manage your time well, you can achieve everything you want in life." That started my quest into the world of time management and learning how to maximise my productivity.

John Foley, barrister, helped me to expand my vision and has inspired me to make possible what seemed impossible. Sherien Foley has always been there to challenge and kickstart me and I remember her words when I hit rock bottom with my work many years ago and she said to me "There's only one way to go and that's up!"

This current series of books about gold grew out of a brainstorming session I had with my old friend, Gail Parr, while staying with her and her husband, George Sansbury at Maryborough in Queensland. We thrashed out the concept and from this grew these five books.

I would also like to acknowledge the late and great Jim Lynch who introduced me to the Charters Towers gold story many years ago and to his, son, Mark Lynch, Chairperson of the Citigold Corporation, who has always supported and encouraged my creativity in relation to the gold story both in books and in art.

And finally, thank you Eddie Dowd, my backstop and mentor, who has helped me get my books into their final form and ready for publication.

Marji Hill

"Asian visitors frequented the northern
Australian coast for a period of several
hundred years to just after
the conclusion of the nineteenth century."

Marji Hill

Chapter 1 — Early Visitors

Prior to 1788 when British ships arrived in Sydney to establish a penal colony, visitors from other countries came to what was regarded as that strange and unknown continent down under. When the first visitors came is open for conjecture.

The first migrants?

For thousands of years, there was contact between the first people of Australia with the people of Papua New Guinea. When the sea levels were low, the two countries - Papua New Guinea and Australia - were connected by land. This was during the Ice Ages.

The people of Papua New Guinea and those of the Torres Strait and the Cape York Peninsula intermarried and exchanged cultural values and technology.

The Chinese

It is possible that the first Chinese visited Australia in the early 1400s.

More than six hundred years ago the Chinese were great travellers and explorers. In the early 1400s between 1405 and 1432, Zheng He (Ch'eng Ho) and his fleet of ships ventured into uncharted waters bordering the Indian Ocean. These places included east Africa, India, Java and Sumatra[1].

The fleet also reached the island of Timor. Australia being only a short distance south of Timor implies that Zheng He may have reached Australia but as yet there is no evidence.

The National Museum Australia[2] refers to a 1477 map that shows the outline of the

---

[1] Hill, Marji (2021) *Australian Aboriginal History: 5 Stories of Indigenous Heroes*. Gold Coast, Qld, The Prison Tree Press, p.6
[2] National Museum Australia https://www.nma.gov.au/explore/features/harvest-of-endurance/scroll/early-chinese-migrants#:~:text=The%20earliest%20known%20Chinese%20immigrant,and%20purchased%20land%20at%20Parramatta.

Australian continent. It also refers to the journal of *HMS Investigator.*

Matthew Flinders had made a note that First Nations people in the Gulf of Carpentaria seemed to know about firearms and iron tools. Flinders reported seeing pieces of earthen jars, bamboo latticework and other articles which he thought to be of Chinese origin.

In 1879 a Chinese statuette from the Ming dynasty was discovered in Darwin. Some porcelain from the same era was found in the Gulf of Carpentaria.

The exact dating of these objects has not been possible. These items could have been brought by the ships in the early 1400s. On the other hand, the Chinese statuette could have been brought by Chinese miners who came to the Northern Territory in 1874 to work on the goldfields.

Theories about the Chinese being early visitors to Australia are unsubstantiated.

Asian trade route

Asian visitors frequented the northern Australian coast for a period of several hundred years to just after the conclusion of the nineteenth century. At least 1,000 Macassans from the Indonesian island of Sulewesi visited northern Australia each year.

These Macassan visitors fished for the sea slug called trepang. Trepang also known as *beche-de-mer,* was a prized delicacy in Chinese cuisine and was the largest Indonesian export to China which was controlled by Chinese merchants living in Macassar [3].

The Macassans processed trepang on Australia's northern shores for the lucrative Chinese market long before the British ever arrived in Australia.

Their visits were part of a great north-south trade route that stretched from China to Australia and back.

---

[3] Mulvaney, D. J. (1969) *The Prehistory of Australia.* London, Thames & Hudson.

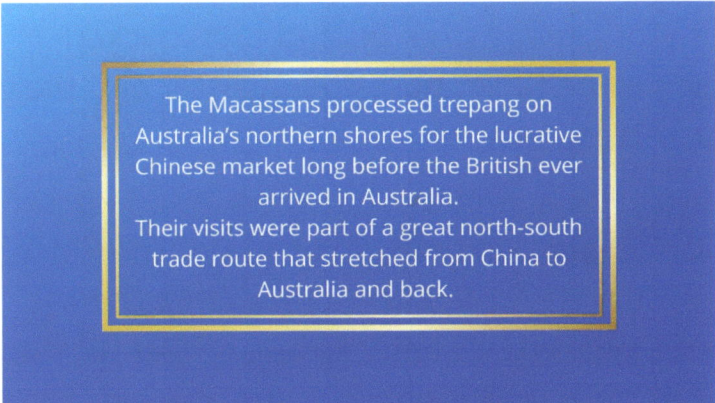

The Macassans processed trepang on Australia's northern shores for the lucrative Chinese market long before the British ever arrived in Australia.
Their visits were part of a great north-south trade route that stretched from China to Australia and back.

Each year, Macassans would visit Australia. They stayed on the northern shores for approximately five months at a time and then they would head back in April of each year to Macassar when the winds changed to the southeast.

Macassans established settlements on the sheltered coastline in Arnhem Land not far from the shallow waters where the trepang was collected. They set up processing plants for the trepang.

They built rows of stone fireplaces which supported the cauldrons in which the trepang was boiled. The second stage of the processing involved burying the trepang in the sand. It was smoked and then packed ready to be taken back to Macassar and the markets in Asia.

A lively trade went on between the Macassans and the local First Nations people. The Yolngu of northeast Arnhem Land exchanged turtle shells, pearl shells and cypress timber for knives, axes and tobacco. Macassan words crept into the local language and the dugout canoe and Macassan pipe were introduced.

The remains of Macassan camps can be seen along the northern coast and are usually marked by tamarind trees which grew from seeds left behind by the Macassan visitors.

In 1907 the Australian government put an end to these visits by the Macassans because they became a threat to the pearling industry.

In 2011 an exhibition held at the Melbourne Museum, developed with the support of Rio Tinto, explored the first recorded history of these trade relations between China and Australia.

It told the fascinating story of the First Nations and Asian trade exchange that went on for several hundred years.

European visitors

Other visitors ventured into Australian waters. In the sixteenth and seventeenth centuries, there were the Portuguese and Spanish navigators.

In 1605 the Spanish navigator, Pedro Fernandes de Queirós claimed Vanuatu thinking it was the great southern land, and Luis Vaez de Torres in 1606 sailed through the waters that now bear his name - the Torres Strait.

In that same year, 1606, the Dutch explored the waters around the northern, western and southern coasts.

Then there was the inspiration of Napoleon Bonaparte as Emperor of the French who carried the French to far corners of the globe.

Between 1771 and 1828 the French sent eight expeditions to Australia to expand their knowledge of the little-known world of Australia and the Pacific.

The People's Republic of China

The population of China in 2022 was over 1.4 billion. This is the largest population of any nation in the world and is equivalent to 18.47% of the world's total population.

China's administrative units are based on a three-tier system, with the nation divided into provinces, counties and townships.

The people in different provinces very often represent entirely different language, ethnic and cultural groups. While most belong to the Han people, there are more than 50 other ethnic groups in China.

The Chinese population in Australia

According to the 2016 Australian Census, there were 509,555 Chinese-born people in Australia. Australia was also home to more than 1.2 million people of Chinese ancestry in its population of 23.4 million.

When gold was discovered in the 1850s Chinese immigration to Australia started in earnest.

It was an era when the Chinese came to Australia to escape the conditions of their own country where there was civil disorder, famine and floods.

Chinese immigrants were also attracted by the discovery of gold in Australia.

In 1861 according to the Colonial Census, there were 38,258 Chinese in Australia representing 3.4 per cent of Australia's then population.

This meant the Chinese at that time were the second-largest immigrant group after those from the British Isles [4].

---

[4] Department of Home Affairs (2018) "China-born Community Information Summary"https://www.homeaffairs.gov.au/mca/files/2016-cis-china.pdf

They settled in rural towns and farming areas such as Parramatta, Liverpool, Wollongong, Maitland and Yass.

Others went to Melbourne and the coastal towns of Victoria, Adelaide, Perth, Queensland and the Northern Territory.

Guangdong province

Most Chinese immigrants came from the Guangdong province, and from Tuishan county in particular.

The capital of Guangdong is Guangzhou which was formerly known as Canton. Cantonese has always been the most widely spoken Chinese language in Australia.

In the 1800s, Tuishan was the headquarters of the Australian Land Clearing Company. This Chinese-run company hired Chinese workers to clear land in Australia.

When the workers got to Australia they had to pay the company money out of their earnings. This was to cover their fares and their other expenses.

Only men migrated to Australia. The colonial government at the time did not allow the Chinese wives and families to join them in Australia.

Neither did companies like the Australian Land Clearing Company. Chinese families had to remain in China so that they could pay back the debts of the Chinese migrants if necessary.

The Guangdong province area was rich in agricultural land with more and more people wanting to live there. The end result was overcrowding. Many Chinese wanted to leave to escape these conditions as well as the poor government.

Young men were encouraged to leave China and travel to other countries where they could make money and then return their prosperity to their families in China.

Chinese Empire

In the 1800s the Chinese Empire began to lose its power. It was based on some people having a lot of wealth and others living very poorly but the poor wanted a better life.

The old Chinese social order had begun to break down.

The European Empires contributed to this breakdown of the Chinese Empire. They wanted to trade with China and they wanted access to China's vast resources.

In the 1700s the Spanish, the Portuguese, and the Dutch started trading with China. The British followed and then the Germans, the French and the Japanese.

The Europeans wanted to operate as freely as possible in China and, to make as much money as possible, pressuring the Chinese to comply.

Suffering

The Chinese government became weaker and weaker. Civil wars broke out, and local warlords ruled over their territories.

Conditions in China, particularly in the south, were difficult. The significant rise in population put pressure on available resources. In addition, there was a conflict with an aggressively expanding West, rebellions, severe floods and famines between the years 1849 and 1887.

Rural families suffered. The government was based in the cities and it held onto power longer there than in the country. This meant there was trouble in the rural areas.

By the 1850s in the provinces of Hunan, Guangxi and Guangdong, armed gangs were attacking villages and towns and robbing people. They killed thousands of people or drove them off their land.

Rich agricultural lands were left empty and unused. Food became scarce.

Given these conditions, many Chinese wanted to migrate to other countries in the hope of getting a better life.

People from some of the minority ethnic groups in China migrated to Australia to escape their discrimination in China.

Early Chinese migrants

The first Chinese to settle in Australia were sailors.

From as early as 1788, with British colonisation, trading ships sailed between Australia and China.

When ships from Australia were in Chinese ports they often hired Chinese sailors to replace sailors who had died or who had deserted ship.

When some of these sailors arrived in Australia they chose to stay in Sydney. They were either paid off or they jumped ship.

Following the lead from the sailors, small numbers of Chinese migrants also came to Australia.

Mak Sai Ying

The first known immigrant to Australia from China was Mak Sai Ying (also known as John Shying). He arrived on the ship *Laurel* in February 1818 as a free settler to New South Wales.

Mak Sai Ying

The first known immigrant to Australia from China was Mak Sai Ying (also known as John Shying). He arrived on the ship *Laurel* in February 1818 as a free settler to New South Wales.

Mak Sai Ying was born c1796 in the Chinese city of Guangdong.

In Sydney, he worked as a carpenter for famous English settler, John Blaxland, whom he met aboard the *Laurel*. He later worked for Elizabeth Macarthur, the wife of Australia's wool industry pioneer, John Macarthur.

Mak Sai Ying became a successful businessman and was granted a licence for a public house in Parramatta and he had several other businesses.

Dr Kate Bagnall[5] from Wollongong University, an expert in early Chinese settlement in Australia, says that the number of Chinese in Australia at the time was very small.

It was unlikely, she said, that there was any discrimination. If there was it was certainly not on the scale of that in the gold rush days when the thousands of migrants obviously became a threat to the British and Europeans.

Mak Sai Ying married Sarah Jane Thompson in 1823, an immigrant lady from Ireland. By this time he went by the name of John Shying. They had four sons.

Shortly before the birth of their fourth child in 1831 he mysteriously returned to China possibly having family obligations back there.

There are no records as to why he did this. One can only surmise that he had a family in China and one in Australia.

John Shying returned to Australia five years later. This was after the death of his wife. He

---

[5] Australian Broadcasting Commission
https://www.abc.net.au/news/2018-06-10/first-chinese-settlers-descendants-reconnect-with-their-roots/9845804

married again in 1842, but his second wife died just a few months later.

"It was the discovery of gold in different parts
of Australia
that attracted large numbers of Chinese
and it was gold that influenced the pattern
of Chinese migration to this country."

Marji Hill

Chapter 2 — Early Chinese Migrants

There were just a few Chinese settlers in Australia prior to the 1840s. They came to Australia primarily as servants, artisans or general labourers.

The transportation of convicts to New South Wales (NSW) ceased in 1840. This caused a shortfall in the labour supply; there was a shortage of workers to do all the jobs that had to be done.

Representations were made to the British government to bring more Chinese to Australia to fill this shortfall in the labour force [6].

---

[6] Mo Yimei (1988) *Harvest of Endurance: a History of the Chinese in Australia 1788-1988* Sydney, Australia-China Friendship Society.
http://www.multiculturalaustralia.edu.au/doc/yimei_1.pdf, p.1

The first group of cheap indentured labourers arrived in October 1848 from Xiamen (Amoy), in China's south-eastern province of Fujian. The 120 men included both indentured or contracted labourers and free emigrants.

Big landowners and other employers began recruiting Chinese workers. With the end of convict transportation, more significant numbers of Chinese men began coming to Australia to work as labourers.

Migration in the 1840s

The 1840s marked the first wave of actual migration.

Because of the tough living conditions in southern China - war, political instability, and environmental conditions - Chinese men wanted to migrate to Australia.

With the Australian need for a labour force, over 3,000 Chinese workers arrived in Sydney between 1848 and 1853. Then more came to Victoria and Queensland.

Indentured labourers were recruited from the Fujian province in China to work as shepherds and irrigation experts for private landowners and the Australian Agricultural Company [7].

Once in Australia Chinese men worked hard. The work that was previously done by convicts was now being done by Chinese labourers.

Chinese workers were employed under contracts of two to five years. Most were rural workers but some worked on the waterside. Others were craftspeople or tradespeople.

The Chinese were given jobs that helped to open up and develop the growing settlement.

They cleared many thousands of hectares of land clearing the bush and preparing the land for the farmer. They had traditional skills in managing water and land. They dug wells and irrigation ditches, introduced vegetables, fruits and crops, turning desert areas into productive gardens [8].

---

[7] Lote Agency (2021) "A Brief History of Chinese Migration to Australia" https://www.loteagency.com.au/a-brief-history-of-chinese-migration-to-australia/
[8] Mo Yimei (1988), p.1

Long columns of Chinese workers could be seen travelling from one location to the next carrying all their belongings. When one work contract was finished they moved on to the next.

By 1850 whole shiploads of Chinese were coming to Australia.

Getting to Australia

Almost a third of the Chinese who came to Australia in the 1800s paid their own passage.

The rest came on credit tickets. This meant they borrowed money for their tickets from moneylenders, bankers, village elders or their own families. They often used their land as security and sometimes even families were put up as security[9].

Resistance to Chinese workers

The pursuit of cheap labour sparked a public protest. There was resistance to this cheap

---

[9] Grassby, Al & Hill, Marji (2000) *Chinese Australians*. South Yarra, Vic, Macmillan, p.16

labour and these sentiments escalated into racist opposition toward the Chinese immigrants.

Sections of the European population resented and questioned the Chinese presence in the colony.

This occurred early in the piece. Just as happened later in the century, this resentment was heavily stirred up by racist opposition toward the Chinese ethnicity.

After gold was discovered in 1851, thousands more Chinese migrated to Australia.

It was the discovery of gold in different parts of Australia that attracted large numbers of Chinese and it was gold that influenced the pattern of Chinese migration to this country.

"As the Chinese population grew sections of the European population resented and questioned their presence in the colony."

Marji Hill

Chapter 3 — Discovery of Gold

When gold was discovered in Australia in 1851 news spread like wildfire around the world. It did not take long before gold fever hit.

By the end 1851, there were thousands digging for gold near Ballarat. The news reverberated everywhere - England, Ireland, Scotland, Europe, China and America. Ships full of gold seekers arrived in Melbourne and headed for the goldfields.

In the years from 1851 to 1860, there was a population explosion in Australia with more than 600,000 people arriving[10]. This

---

[10] "A history of the Department of Immigration: managing migration to Australia." https://www.homeaffairs.gov.au/about-us-subsite/files/immigration-history.pdf,p.5

population growth intensified with thousands coming to Australia to seek their fortune.

In 1851 the Australian population was 437,655. A decade later the Australian population was over one million, and the Victorian population had increased to well over half a million.

This rapid growth was predominantly the result of the gold rushes.

When the news reached China about the discovery of gold, almost 40,000 Chinese travelled to the Victorian goldfields by ship.

Chinese migrants

In the first six months of 1852 over 3000 gold seekers had arrived from China. By the end of that year, the numbers had more than doubled with the Chinese coming to their "New Gold Mountain".

In the decade to 1861, the Australian population was 3.3% Chinese. Those 38,258 people had been born in China[11]. This number, according to the National Museum of Australia was not to be equalled until the late 1980s.

Bonded labour

Most Chinese gold seekers came from the Pearl River Delta in southern China. They were desperate to do whatever it took to improve their life.

As mentioned, many who came were contracted by agents who sponsored their journey to Australia. It was a credit ticket system that bonded their labour.

This meant that the cost of their travel was a mortgage against a family or clan land. This bound them to their creditor until either their passage was paid with interest or a specified period had elapsed.

---

[11] National Museum of Australia "Chinese gold miners" https://www.nma.gov.au/explore/features/harvest-of-endurance/scroll/chinese-gold-miners#:~:text=There%20were%20over%2011%2C000%20Chinese,%2C%20Tambaroora%2C%20Tamworth%20and%20Tumut.

A man would take a loan from a local trader, agreeing to send regular repayments. The family who stayed in China would end up working for the trader if the man was unable to repay the loan.

Chinese men were sent to places like Australia and once in Australia, they had to send money back to China.

If they weren't sponsored, Chinese migrants had to raise their own money for their passage to Australia.

Chinese men involuntarily[12] left their wives and families in China. They travelled to the goldfields dreaming of a better life together with the hope of being able to support their families back in China.

A tough life

But life was not easy on the goldfields. It was hard work and it was harsh. The Chinese experienced racial hostility, discrimination and

---

[12] Refer Page 11 herein "The colonial government at the time did not allow the Chinese wives and families to join them in Australia as well as the bond conditions for purchasing passage."

prejudice from the Europeans[13]. When they were successful at obtaining gold, jealousies arose.

The Chinese worked together in teams on the goldfields supervised by a headman. Usually, they came from the same village in China.

The Chinese were hardworking, quiet and law-abiding, dutifully meeting their responsibilities in repaying their ticket credit debts by sending their money back to China.

The Chinese method of gold mining was to rework old claims that had been abandoned by the Europeans. When alluvial gold was running out they would then collect the gold that had been missed from previously worked claims.

The Chinese were entrepreneurial and they sought out opportunities to make money. They provided services to support those living on the diggings: washing clothes, setting up

---

[13] "A Brief History of Chinese Migration to Australia" (2021) https://www.loteagency.com.au/a-brief-history-of-chinese-migration-to-australia/

market gardens, selling cooked food, and supplying herbal medicines.

> **The Chinese method of gold mining was to rework old claims that had been abandoned by the Europeans. When alluvial gold was running out they would then collect the gold that had been missed from previously worked claims.**

As the Chinese population grew, sections of the European population resented and questioned their presence in the colony.

Hardship on the goldfields

There was a lot of hardship on the goldfields. They were dangerous places. Living conditions were cramped.

The rough conditions with people living in tents and shanties meant there were few comforts. Tensions surfaced and fights broke out, often over claim jumping.

In the multicultural melting pot of the Ballarat goldfield, there was plenty of rivalry and fighting. Early in the piece, racism was rife and anti-Chinese sentiment grew.

Gold exports

Most Victorian gold was exported to Britain though a significant amount was sent to the ports in Asia.

Shipping records as early as 1855 show the Chinese transporting gold on vessels that travelled to Hong Kong[14]. From there it was then sent on to destinations in Guangdong and Fujian provinces.

From 1851 to 1860 the Victorian goldfields were the focus of attention in Australia. Until the discovery of gold in north Queensland

---

[14] Guoth, Nicholas & Macgregor, Paul (2019) "Getting Chinese Gold off the Victorian Goldfields" Chinese Southern Diaspora Studies, 8: 134.

later in the century, Victoria was Australia's most important gold producer.

Gold! Hidden Stories of Australia's Past,
Book 3

"Australian Parliament, just days after federation in 1901,
was to pass the Immigration Restriction Act.
Here was the White Australia Policy,
shaped by decades of anti-Chinese sentiment extending back to the goldfields."

Tony Wright

Chapter 4 — Anti-Chinese Legislation

When news about the discoveries of gold of 1851 reached China, thousands of Chinese were soon migrating to the Australian goldfields.

In the 1830s and early 1840s, exposure to Chinese migrants was low and so they were of little concern.

This changed in the 1850s. From the European perspective, it seemed as though the Chinese were arriving on the Australian goldfields at an alarming rate.

By mid-1855 around 17,000 Chinese were on the goldfields. By 1861, nearly 40,000 Chinese had arrived.

Given the flood of Chinese to the goldfields it was not long before resentment and ill-feeling grew.

The Chinese question became a subject of hot debate both on the goldfields and beyond. The response by the colonial government was to implement poll taxes and restrictions to limit the number of Chinese entering Australia.

Both New South Wales (NSW) and Victoria commenced immigration restrictions.

The mass migration of the Chinese to Australia was seen as a security risk. The colonial government feared what might be the possible intentions of the Chinese emperor. In addition, they feared competition on the goldfields.

Even though the Chinese miners reworked old claims that had been deserted by the Europeans these actions still upset the Europeans. The Chinese were accused of taking their claims and disgruntled diggers blamed the Chinese for all their misfortunes.

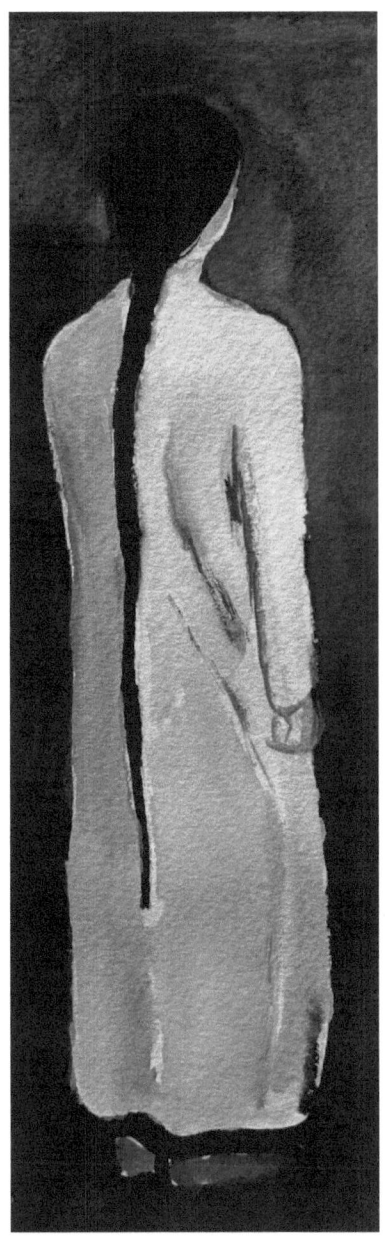

The Chinese looked very different to the Europeans

1855 Anti-Chinese legislation

Anti-Chinese legislation - the *Chinese Restriction Act* - was passed by the Victorian government in 1855. This legislation was a first both for Australia and the British colonial world.

A tax of £10 was placed on every Chinese person arriving in the colony. Restrictions were designed to limit the number of Chinese permitted to disembark from ships arriving in Melbourne.

There was to be just one Chinese person for every 10 tonnes of shipping. Protectors were appointed to regulate Chinese activity and to shield them from attacks by the Europeans.

From this time on the Victorian government made various attempts to restrict the number of Chinese arriving in the colony. Not only was there the £10 immigration tax, but the Chinese were forced to live in special villages set apart from the other miners.

> **Anti-Chinese legislation - the Chinese Restriction Act - was passed by the Victorian government in 1855. This legislation was a first both for Australia and the British colonial world.**

The Victorian anti-Chinese legislation was followed by similar legislation in NSW after the major race riot at Lambing Flat of 1860-61.

These laws were the precursor of the federal *Immigration Restriction Act* of 1901 - the Act that merged into the White Australia Policy which excluded non-European migration to Australia right up until the 1970s.

Robe

To bypass these restrictions in Victoria, the Chinese instead travelled to South Australia. They disembarked at the small town of Robe located hundreds of kilometres away from the Victorian goldfields.

Robe became the new port of call for the Chinese wanting to travel to the goldfields. Others got off their ships in Sydney and walked to the goldfields in NSW.

The Chinese that arrived at Robe had to travel hundreds of kilometres to the goldfields. They either walked or travelled by coach. This journey which took weeks added to their hardships in Australia [15].

The trek from Robe to the Victorian goldfields took at least three weeks and often more. If they walked to NSW the walk, of course, was even longer.

Walking to the goldfields was not without danger. They could be ambushed by

---

[15] Webber, Kimberley (2012) *Growing Up on the Goldfields*. South Yarra, Vic., Macmillan Education, p. 26

bushrangers. Words in Chinese were sometimes written up on trees to warn others of impending danger. Signs were put up giving directions to mining camps and fellow citizens[16].

Often the Chinese walked in single file in groups of up to 700 carrying their belongings in baskets hanging from bamboo poles. Travelling in large parties gave better protection from bushrangers.

Between 1857 and 1862 a total of 35 ships with around 16,500 Chinese gold-seekers had arrived at Robe[17].

Protest

Chinese miners responded to the immigration restrictions and the discriminatory practices

---

[16] Fung, Pamie (2015) "The significance of the first anti-Chinese legislation in Australia" https://peril.com.au/topics/politics/anti-chinese-legislation-in-australia/

[17] Brown, Cash "The treks from Robe" https://victoriancollections.net.au/media/exhibitions/5fbd874fd5fa8108043fc293//5fc8d9e89992142684f04d6a/original.pdf

Gold! Hidden Stories of Australia's Past, Book 3

with civil disobedience. There were protests and petitions.

In November 1857, the Victorian government passed an Act that required all Chinese residing in Victoria to obtain a £1 license which had to be renewed every two months for an additional £1 in order to remain in the colony of Victoria.

Anti-Chinese sentiment heightened with the increasing presence of Chinese miners on the Victorian goldfields. Anti-Chinese riots were an outcome of these taking place on several Victorian goldfields.

The worst occurrence took place in north-eastern Victoria in the Buckland Valley on 4 July 1857.

Then in 1859, when the Chinese population on the goldfields escalated, even more, there was further protest.

Chinese Residence Tax Revolt of 1859

1859 saw the Chinese Residence Tax Revolt in Victoria when more than 33,000 Chinese miners refused to pay the tax. Chinese were fined and jailed and rebellion at the time was a real possibility.

Since 1855 the Victorian government had made various attempts to restrict the number of Chinese gold miners entering the country with its £10 immigration tax, the protectorate system of Chinese-only settlements and discriminatory mining taxes which charged higher rates for Chinese miners.

Paul Macgregor[18] who explores this Tax Revolt likens it to the battle of the Eureka Stockade of 1854, in terms of miners demanding rights and fair treatment.

Chinese diggers protested against the poll tax. They formed the 'United Confederacy of Chinese' on the Ovens, Bendigo, Castlemaine and Ballarat goldfields.

By 1859, this protest came to a head when several thousand Chinese people marched in protest in Castlemaine. They presented a

---

[18] Eureka Centre Ballarat (2022)"Ballarat Harmony Fest - the Chinese Miners' 'Residence Tax Revolt' of 1859"
https://www.eurekacentreballarat.com.au/ballarat-harmony-fest-chinese-miners-residence-tax-revolt-1859

petition containing many thousands of signatures in support of their cause to the Victorian Government.

Why did anti-Chinese sentiment grow?

First of all, the Chinese looked very different to the Europeans.

Chinese man carrying his load hanging from bamboo poles carried across his shoulders

They had pigtails. They wore strange, conical-shaped hats and long garments which resembled women's clothing or else they wore blue padded jackets, wide pantaloons, and white socks.

If they were not barefoot they wore thick rope sole shoes.

A typical sight was Chinese men carrying loads hanging from bamboo poles carried across their shoulders.

Different customs

Secondly, the Chinese had their own religious practices and different customs - all strange to the Europeans.

Not only did the Chinese work together in teams they also lived and ate together in separate settlements.

It was rare ever to find women living and working with them.

This all-male predominance of Chinese men on the goldfields was another cause of suspicion and ill-feeling.

Gold mining successes

Third, the Chinese were often successful at digging for gold. They were productive. When Chinese miners discovered gold at Ararat the news was treated with jealousy and anger from the other miners.

Where the Europeans mostly worked alone on the goldfields the Chinese worked in groups.

It was not the usual practice for the Chinese to open up new mining areas. The reworked old claims. They knew how to carefully use and preserve water.

The skills that helped the Chinese to be successful at gold prospecting were often too difficult for the Europeans.

Conflict

As the Chinese became a perceived threat to the Anglo establishment and were seen to be in competition with the European miners, conflict developed.

Even though the Chinese only reworked claims that had been abandoned by the

Europeans, they could still be accused of taking their claims.

Sometimes the Chinese were driven off if claims were found to be rich in gold.

At Bendigo, police had to guard Chinese camps. European miners were threatened with arrest if they took violent action against the Chinese and special Chinese constables and interpreters were employed to protect them.

1861 Chinese Immigrants Regulation and Restriction Act

In November 1861 the NSW Government passed the *Chinese Immigrants Regulation and Restriction Act*. Again, this was designed to limit the numbers of Chinese in the colony and was a tariff for Chinese people only.

Anti-Chinese sentiment continued to grow. By the 1880s it was very strong in New South Wales.

The *Chinese Restriction and Regulation Act* of 1888 was passed to protect the colony from the dangers of Chinese immigration.

In 1889 the *Immigration Restriction Act* required anyone wanting to migrate to NSW to write out a passage in a 'European language'. This was chosen by the immigration officer. It could be ANY European language[19].

1901 Immigration Restriction Act

In 1901 the new federal government passed the *Immigration Restriction Act.* It retained the clause that anyone migrating to Australia had to write out a passage in a European language to be allowed to enter.

This 1901 Act was the beginning of what is now known as the White Australia Policy which was shaped by decades of anti-Chinese sentiment extending back to the discovery of gold[20].

---

[19] Washington, Edward "Chinese on the Goldfields" Sydney Living Museums https://sydneylivingmuseums.com.au/stories/chinese-goldfields#:~:text=In%201901%20the%20now%20federal,to%20be%20allowed%20to%20enter.

[20] Wright, Tony (2020) "A thorny trail from Buckland to our battles with Beijing" The Age, December 5

It defined Australia's international stance, a position based on institutional racism towards the first group of non-European immigrants to Australia.

It remained the policy for Australia for many decades until it was dismantled by the Whitlam government and replaced with the policy of multiculturalism in 1973.

Goldfield rioting

The reaction to the presence of Chinese miners on the Victorian and NSW goldfields grew; the fear of the "yellow peril," the hoards from the north, stimulated institutional racism with the implementation of anti-Chinese legislation ultimately leading to the White Australia policy.

Not only at the government level but antagonism and hostility surfaced within the ranks of the European miners. Violent attacks against the Chinese were commonplace.

At Bendigo on 8 July, 1854, an estimated 1,500 European miners met at a hotel in Bendigo with plans to drive out the Chinese.

Three years later Chinese were attacked in the Buckland Valley goldfields - this event became known as the Buckland Valley Riot.

Gold! Hidden Stories of Australia's Past,
Book 3

"The accounts of anti-Chinese violence at Buckland River in Victoria in 1857 and at Lambing Flat in 1860-61 in NSW, illustrate the brutality with which European miners could treat Chinese miners on the goldfields."

Pamie Fung

Chapter 5 — Buckland Valley

The Buckland Valley Riot happened on 4 July 1857 when tensions between at least 2,000 Chinese and hundreds of European miners erupted.

Buckland Valley, the land of the Yaitmathang people, is near Bright in north-eastern Victoria. In the gold rush days, diggers there mined for alluvial gold.

A European land owner, Thomas Buckland, settled in the district in 1845.

An American, Harry Pardoe, first started digging in the area in 1853. Within

four years, the area had become known as Buckland and had a population of at least 6,000 people, possibly more, as easily accessible alluvial gold discoveries were abundant.

When gold began to peter out Chinese miners moved in. This was because their method of mining for gold was to rework claims that had been abandoned by the Europeans.

When there were only a few Chinese miners in the Buckland Valley anti-Chinese feelings were not an issue.

Chinese were recognised as industrious workers. They were highly skilled at reworking old claims, they were well organised, and they could extract gold successfully.

But as easy gold petered out more and more Chinese miners moved into the Buckland Valley.

This, coupled with their appearance, their different customs and their eating habits, led to envy and many false rumours about their successes.

Stories circulated about the Chinese smoking opium, gambling and getting women for prostitution.

Rumours led to ill-feeling towards the Chinese; they became hated, and this eventually led to aggression.

The Chinese miners sunk sophisticated mineshafts. They were successful at what they did. They set up a flourishing settlement and had their own stores and a place of worship.

Chinese temple

The Europeans at the time found themselves in the minority because so many Chinese had moved onto the goldfield.

Attitudes towards the Chinese were volatile and hostile. Anger flared. Anti-Chinese placards appeared calling for all Chinese to be driven off the goldfields.

The Europeans would claim-jump profitable Chinese mines. They aggressively attacked them, beating them, stoning them and cutting off their pigtails.

If any Europeans were arrested and taken off to court for anti-Chinese behaviour, European juries returned verdicts of not guilty.

Violence erupts

Violence erupted on American Independence Day, 4 July 1857. On this day a group of English, Irish, Germans and Americans attacked the Chinese settlements.

On that fateful morning at the local hotel a group of Americans, drunk from their celebrations, left the Buckland Hotel, took matters into their own hands and joined others determined to remove the Chinese from the Buckland Valley. Intoxicated with alcohol they took up picks, axe handles and lumps of wood and joined the attacking party to drive the Chinese away.

Valley of death

A riot took place.

Chinese miners were beaten, robbed and their property was destroyed by the so-called aggrieved European diggers. Chinese were herded across the river and driven away.

Mayhem reigned. Tents were looted, torn down and torched. A tent with four Chinese inside was set alight but tragedy was averted with the arrival of police.

The newly-constructed temple was torched and burnt to ashes.

All along the Buckland Valley the Chinese were beaten as they escaped. Three Chinese miners were reported to have died as they fled the area.

Aitchison[21] refers to rumours of a massacre that took place at Buckland Valley on that day. Rumour also has it that hundreds of Chinese were slaughtered and thrown down

---

[21] Aitchison, James (2019) "Non-fiction: madness and massacre: Chinese miners on the Victorian Goldfields" Storgy Magazine in Arts & Culture, Non-Fiction, January.
https://storgy.com/2019/01/17/non-fiction-madness-and-massacre-chinese-miners-on-the-victorian-goldfields-by-james-aitchison/

mineshafts. There were other reports of sightings of decomposed bodies.

What is definite is that on that day European diggers attacked the Chinese and drove them from the area.

> **A RIOT TOOK PLACE**
> Chinese miners were beaten, they were robbed, and their property was destroyed by the so-called aggrieved European diggers. Chinese were herded across the river and driven away.

How many Chinese actually died no one knows.

Aitchison[22] says that what appeared to be a massacre was downplayed by the authorities. The three reported deaths were attributed to "exposure, cold and previous illness."

---

[22] Aitchison, James, *ibid*

Other stories were that the Chinese were left to die in the forest, were thrown down mine shafts or were drowned in their desperation to escape their attackers.

Twelve Europeans were charged with the riot. When they faced trial in Beechworth, an anti-Chinese Immigration League raised funds for their defence.

Chinese witnesses were discredited. Rioters and their friends provided alibis for one another and juries in most cases returned verdicts of not guilty. Only three of them were given light sentences.

Robert O`Hara Burke (of Burke and Wills fame), who was working as a policeman at Beechworth, was sent to help restore law and order.

All signs of what happened that day have been brushed away with time, and there are no remains of the reportedly beautiful Chinese temple.

A monument commemorates the riot that took place in the Buckland Valley and today it is a peaceful place of orchards, farms and vineyards.

As alluvial gold disappeared, Buckland Valley moved first of all to reef mining and later to dredging. By the early years of the twentieth century, the area had outlived its usefulness. The village was eventually removed.

According to Monument Australia, many details of the Buckland Valley riot are still debated as court records have mysteriously disappeared from the Beechworth Court House [23].

The anti-Chinese violence at Buckland River in 1857 and then again at Lambing Flat in 1860-61 in NSW, is testimony to the brutality with which European diggers could treat Chinese miners on the goldfields[24].

---

[23] Monument Australia https://monumentaustralia.org.au/themes/government/dissent/display/30547-buckland-riot

[24] Fung, Pamie (2015) "The significance of the first anti-Chinese legislation in Australia" https://peril.com.au/topics/politics/anti-chinese-legislation-in-australia/

Gold! Hidden Stories of Australia's Past,
Book 3

What took place at Lambing Flat
in New South Wales in June 1861
"was one of the most horrific explosions
of racial violence in Australian history."

Mo Yimei

Chapter 6 — Lambing Flat

What took place at Lambing Flat in New South Wales (NSW) in June 1861 in the view of Mo Yimei[25] "was one of the most horrific explosions of racial violence in Australian history."

As was the battle of the Eureka Stockade in 1854, this anti-Chinese riot was another defining moment in Australia's past the implications of which reverberated throughout Australian political and cultural history.

The Lambing Flat riot was not an isolated expression of aggression against the Chinese in New South Wales.

---

[25] Mo Yimei (1988) *Harvest of Endurance: a History of the Chinese in Australia 1788-1988* Sydney, Australia-China Friendship Society.
http://www.multiculturalaustralia.edu.au/doc/yimei_1.pdf

Anti-Chinese tensions had surfaced in other NSW areas [26]:

- Turon River (1853) was the site of one of Australia's first alluvial gold rushes, where Chinese migrant workers built a water race to bring water to mining operations in the area. Violence erupted here between miners and licensing authorities during the gold rush;

- Meroo (1854) Central West region of NSW;

- Rocky River (1856) near Uralla on the New England Tableland was a gold mining area with an estimated 4,000 to 5,000 miners including many Chinese, some of whom had made the long trek from Goulburn and the Victorian goldfields;

- Tambaroora (1858) Central Tablelands of NSW in the region of Orange, Bathurst and Mudgee. The Chinese arrived on the goldfield in 1856 which initially drew a

---

[26] Thompson, S. (2011) "1860 Lambing Flat *Roll Up* Banner" Sydney, Migration Heritage Centre, Power House Museum. https://www.migrationheritage.nsw.gov.au/exhibition/objectsthroughtime/lambingflatsbanner/index.html

great deal of negativity from the European mining community;

- Kiandra (1860) is situated in the Snowy Mountains region 90 kilometres north-west of Cooma. In November 1859, gold was discovered and some 10,000 miners and storekeepers descended on the area including significant numbers of Chinese;

- Nundle (1861) in the New England region of NSW not far from Tamworth. Gold was discovered in 1852 at Hanging Rock. Villages in the area flourished with thousands of miners and prospectors coming from different parts of the world including China;

- Tingha tin fields (1870) near Armidale on the New England Tableland where around 5,000 people arrived including around 1,000 Chinese.

Young, NSW

In 1861, the town of Young in NSW was known as Lambing Flat. It was renamed

"Young" in 1863 and is situated on the southwest slopes region of NSW, approximately a two-hour drive from Canberra.

It is home to the Burrowmunditory people, a clan of the Wiradjuri.

Gold had been discovered in this region in 1860.

As happened on other goldfields in NSW and Victoria the discovery of gold in the Young district attracted thousands of miners and prospectors.

This goldfield was rich. It was easy to work and involved limited investment and manpower. Competition for the gold, however, was huge.

Discrimination against the Chinese in Victoria by the colonial authorities was rife so with the anti-Chinese legislation of 1855 many Chinese moved across the border into New South Wales. Apart from those that came from Victoria, large numbers of Chinese had also arrived in Sydney. Their destination was Lambing Flat.

Chinese at Lambing Flat

Mo Yimei[27] says Chinese miners were enticed to Lambing Flat in gangs of up to 200 young men with promises of rich rewards for working the goldfields.

As happened during this gold rush era Chinese men were recruited by enterprising merchants in Sydney, Melbourne and Hong Kong. Most came to Australia on the credit-ticket system.

To summarise again, their fares from Southern China were paid and in return, the Chinese had their living expenses paid. The Chinese migrants then had to give a small percentage of the gold they found to their sponsors until such time as the cost of their travel to Australia had been recouped.

The unsuspecting Chinese men would land in Sydney and Melbourne and walk to the goldfields.

---

[27] Mo Yimei, *ibid,* p.2

Once in the country, they were monitored by headmen or bosses in association with fraternal organisations[28].

When they reached their destinations the sponsors organised an extensive social network surrounding these men, securing their employment and taking care of their needs, as well as ensuring their financial obligations were met.

The British and European miners on the goldfields were already doing it tough. When the Chinese arrived, resentment arose as the Chinese were seen as a threat to their livelihood.

Chinese workers

As already seen on the other goldfields in NSW and Victoria, Chinese miners were highly organised and worked in teams, each of which had a leader.

---

[28] . McGowan, Barry "The Braidwood district's Chinese heritage" Braidwood & District Historical Society. http://braidwoodmuseum.org.au/Chinese.html

The Chinese way of gold mining was different to that of the Europeans who tended to work alone or in small groups.

Generally, the Chinese were willing immigrants, peaceful and industrious. They worked well in groups and much of their success was attributed to this method of prospecting for gold.

Culturally different

But the Chinese were distrusted.

The Europeans didn't like their dress, customs or traditions[29]. They disliked their habits of opium smoking, gambling and their religion aroused suspicion — Chinese religion was different to the Christians; they were devout Buddhists or Taoists.

They looked so very different with their long pigtails, wooden-soled shoes and wide-

---

[29] Thompson, S. (2011) https://www.migrationheritage.nsw.gov.au/exhibition/objectsthroughtime/lambingflatsbanner/index.html)

brimmed straw hats. Their food was different. They spoke a different language.

As with the prevailing attitudes of the nineteenth century, the Europeans had their own ideas about what was considered cultural superiority. The Chinese, together with the First Nations people, were considered racially inferior.

The Chinese groups had their own mining infrastructure[30]. For their own needs, they built waterways and dams and this was another source of tension.

Water was in short supply and Chinese mining methods involved the heavy use of water and they muddied the water that was needed for washing gold. Despite cautions on their water usage, the Chinese persisted with their own way of operating.

Chinese mining efforts in the main were successful except their fate was not always one of success. Thousands returned to China.

---

[30] CBHS Year 5 History
http://cbhsyearfivehistory.weebly.com/chinese-miner-riots.html

Some are known to have developed severe mental issues. Others experienced extreme poverty. Then there were those who continued to search for gold at the expense of their lives[31].

Europeans would abandon a claim if it appeared to be unproductive. The Chinese would then rework these claims.

The Chinese would sift through the mining rubble and tailings which Europeans needed to fall back on in times of their own hardship.

One of the characteristics of the Chinese miners was persistence. They often found a lot of gold on the claims that the Europeans had abandoned.

This made the Europeans jealous and full of resentment. They accused the Chinese of taking their gold and fear, anger and wild rumours fuelled animosity.

These tensions led to an explosive situation.

---

[31] Fung, Pamie (2015) "The significance of the first anti-Chinese legislation in Australia" https://peril.com.au/topics/politics/anti-chinese-legislation-in-australia/

Racial tension

By late 1860 and early into 1861 European miners had made several attacks on Chinese miners in the Lambing Flat area.

An initial disturbance grew out of a demonstration organised by a European miners vigilance committee against gambling dens and other so-called vices on December 12, 1860[32].

The miners vented their anger at these establishments and they attacked the Chinese settlement.

The Europeans expressed their hatred of the Chinese justifying their brutality by claiming that the Chinese were squandering the water supply so vital to alluvial prospecting. They burned Chinese tents and destroyed their provisions. Some of the Chinese miners were driven away.

---

[32] Britannica "Lambing Flat Riots"
https://www.britannica.com/event/Lambing-Flat-Riots)

As there were no troopers stationed at Lambing Flat there was no colonial policing to control law and order.

Angry anti-Chinese miners met at the *All and Ale* pub at Tipperary Gully. They wanted the Chinese off the goldfields.

They designed and carried their own banner with the words, "Roll up Roll up No Chinese."

The anti-Chinese Roll Up banner

The Roll Up Banner

The Roll Up banner was a cloth banner with a hand-painted Southern Cross emblem. Around the outside was painted the slogan 'Roll Up, Roll Up, No Chinese' [33].

The banner was made of white cotton with yellow, red and blue paint.

Like the Southern Cross flag, the Roll Up banner is one of the oldest banners in Australian history.

It symbolises the story of the Chinese on the goldfields. It's a symbol of the myths surrounding the Chinese which provided the seeds for the political ideology and institutionalised racism which was behind the 1901 White Australia policy.

The banner represents the ever-present undercurrent of racism in Australian history.

---

[33] Thompson, S. (2011) "1860 Lambing Flat *Roll Up* Banner" Sydney, Migration Heritage Centre, Power House Museum. https://www.migrationheritage.nsw.gov.au/exhibition/objectsthroughtime/lambingflatsbanner/index.html

Rioting

On 30 June 1861, European men began to gather with bludgeons and pick- handles. The cry was 'No Chinese'. A local band played as they marched on Lambing Flat[34].

The gathering swelled to at least 1,000 European agitators, maybe a lot more. On that day they invaded all the Chinese camps in the area, burning and destroying them, and taking over not just the town but the entire area.

On that fateful day, they marched from Tipperary Gully and attacked two of the main Chinese camps at Blackguard Gully and Back Creek. Forewarned, the Chinese diggers had headed for the goldfields. Their empty camp was torn apart. Tents, supplies, clothing and furniture were torched and mining tools destroyed.

Mo Yimei[35] describes how some Europeans on horseback managed to round up a thousand or more Chinese like cattle and the mob went to work with appalling hatred.

---

[34] Mo Yimei, *ibid*, p. 2
[35] Mo Yimei, *ibid*, p.3

The Chinese were mercilessly beaten and whipped, their dwellings plundered and their possessions piled into huge bonfires. Miners on horseback overtook the fleeing Chinese and degraded, beat and robbed them.

Chinese men were brutally attacked and even scalped. They cut off their pigtails returning with pigtails cut or torn from their owner's heads hanging from their belts like Indian scalps.

On that cold, winter night, the Chinese were expelled with no equipment and no provisions.

Aftermath

Following the riot, over one thousand Chinese took shelter at a local landowner's property.

The property, *Currawong*, was that of James Roberts which was 20 kilometres away near Murrumburrah. Roberts, his wife Elizabeth, and their employees fed and sheltered the Chinese for two weeks.

A week following the riot, military arrived on Lambing Flat. These were the soldiers from the East Suffolk Regiment (12th) with armed auxiliaries that went into action between the Chinese and European diggers.

The ringleaders of the riot were arrested on 14 July but there was further protest.

One thousand diggers attacked the police station to free their men. The outcome was one death when the police fired and charged the crowd. The next day the men were released.

The riot led the assistant gold commissioner to read the British Parliament's Riot Act of 1714, which gave local authorities the power to declare a group of twelve or more people to be an unlawful assembly and order them to disperse or face punishment.

Reaction in the colony to what happened at Lambing Flat was one of shock, but local opinion said it was all to do with the presence of the Chinese.

The shame of Lambing Flat was such that its name was soon changed to Young in honour of the Governor of NSW [36].

> **The landscape of Young remains haunted by the hollowed-out goldfields but the bloodshed of the Lambing Flat riots, as they became known, has been largely subsumed in the myths that Australia tells of its birth and nationhood.**
>
> **Lauren Carroll Harris**

The government, moved by public opinion to follow the Victorian example, in November 1861 took steps to restrict the number of the Chinese in the State.

---

[36] Harris, Lauren Carroll (2018) "The riots history erased: reckoning with the racism of Lambing Flat" The Guardian, 7 August
https://www.theguardian.com/artanddesign/2018/aug/07/the-riots-history-erased-reckoning-with-the-racism-of-lambing-flat

Anti-Chinese legislation

The NSW government's response to events at Lambing Flat was the passing of the anti-Chinese immigration Act in November 1861 – the *Chinese Immigrants Regulation and Restriction Act*.

This Act was designed to limit the numbers of Chinese in the colony and to limit where the Chinese could mine. This was part of the evolution leading to the White Australia Policy which aimed at restricting non-European immigration.

"Anti-Chinese attitudes and the fear of competition on the goldfields resulted in discriminatory legislation - the 1855 Act and future legislation - which can only be described as institutionalised racism."

Marji Hill

Chapter 7 — Expanding Frontiers

In the second half of the nineteenth century prior to Federation in 1901, thousands of Chinese had migrated to Australia. In the decades 1850 to 1870 most Chinese immigrants worked on goldfields in New South Wales (NSW) and Victoria.

In the latter part of the nineteenth century, Chinese miners migrated to North Queensland and the Northern Territory. Some went to northern Tasmania and others to Western Australia.

Queensland frontier

By 1870 many Chinese went to Queensland in search of gold.

Gold was discovered at Charters Towers (136 kilometres southwest of Townsville) by First Nations horse boy, Jupiter Mosman on Christmas Eve in 1871.

Around a year later it was found on the Palmer River. Then at Croydon in 1886.

Gold mining in Queensland had begun at Canoona in 1858. This stimulated the discovery of gold at Gympie in 1867.

Following these gold discoveries, the Chinese rushed to the northern frontier.

Chinese in Queensland

The pioneer of Chinese business in Queensland was Andrew Leon. He wasn't a gold miner; he worked in tropical agriculture. His business was the 'Hap Wah plantation Company' - the First Sugar growing venture in Cairns in 1878 [37].

---

[37] Rutian, Mi (2020)"Chinese Business History in Queensland - Gold rush: 1851-1881" State Library of Queensland https://www.slq.qld.gov.au/blog/chinese-business-history-queensland-gold-rush-1851-1881)

At the height of the gold rush in North Queensland, there were thousands of Chinese on the goldfield but not all of them prospected for gold. Many grew vegetables, got into the banana industry, grew sugar cane, cooked meals, ran general stores, or offered specialist services like herbal medicine.

Cooktown was the arrival port for many of the Chinese coming into North Queensland.

The adverse resentment of the Chinese that found expression down south in Victoria and NSW continued onto the Queensland goldfields.

In 1877, the Queensland government passed *The Chinese Immigrants Regulation Act* designed to restrict Chinese. This authorised a ten-pound poll tax to be paid by ships' masters on every Chinese person transported on their vessels.

By this time the Chinese mining population had peaked to over 18,000 outnumbering European alluvial gold miners.

There were probably more Chinese on the Palmer River than Europeans in the entire northern half of Australia [38].

In 1883 half if not more of the populations of the Cairns, Port Douglas, Innisfail and Atherton regions were of Chinese descent.

Chinese and First Nations

Part of the untold and hidden history of Australia is the interrelationship between the Chinese and First Nations people.

The historical connections between these two marginalised groups started when the Chinese started migrating to Australia.

Both the Chinese and First Nations people experienced discrimination and prejudice, and each were victim of massacre, brutality and were despised.

---

[38] Burke, Heather & Grimwade, Gordon (2013) The Historical Archaeology of the Chinese in Far North Queensland Vol. 16 https://www.academia.edu/7250100/Historical_Archaeology_of_the_Chinese_in_far_north_Queensland p. 121

Dr Sandi Robb[39] is one researcher who has analysed the relationships and marriage patterns between Chinese men and First Nation women in North Queensland.

There was a degree of rapport between both cultural groups. They had similar social and cultural features such as clans and a social system that was based on kinship.

Given that Chinese men migrated to Australia and left their wives and families back in China, Chinese men sometimes struck up liaisons with First Nation women.

These relationships were disapproved of by colonial authorities.

Robb[40] refers to the fact that despite this disapproval some Chinese/First Nation relationships did happen which resulted in families of Chinese and First Nations descent.

Compared to the number of Chinese men that married European women in the second half of the nineteenth century the number of

---

[39] Robb, Sandi (2019) *North Queensland's Chinese Family Landscape: 1860-1920.* PhD Thesis, p. 218

[40] Robb, *Ibid*, p.202

marriages between Chinese men and First Nations women was low.

Most children of these relationships identified with their First Nations ancestry and given this heritage these children could be taken away by government authorities. Some of these descendants became part of the Stolen Generations.

Tommy Ah Toy and his First Nation wife had a son who was born around 1912. In 1922 the boy became a Stolen Generation victim when he was removed by a Laura policeman on a Government Removal Order and despatched to Yarrabah Mission Station[41].

Jason Wing[42] is a Sydney-based artist of Chinese and First Nations descent. His artwork reflects the legacy of his Chinese and First

---

[41] Jack, Ian; Holmes, Kate, and Kerr, Ruth (1984) "Ah Toy's Garden: A Chinese Market-Garden on the Palmer River Goldfield, North Queensland" Australian Historical Archaeology, 2: 52 (http://www.asha.org.au/pdf/australasian_historical_archaeology/02_04_Jack.pdf)

[42] Yang, Eugene (2018) "Chinese and Indigenous Australians share a long, 'untold history' that's been captured through art" https://www.abc.net.au/news/2018-06-23/indigenous-and-chinese-relationship-in-australian-history/9893920

Nations heritage. His maternal grandfather, Bill Irving, was part of the Stolen Generation.

JASON WING
Artist
Sydney-based artist of Chinese and First Nations descent.
His artworks reflect the legacy of his Chinese and First Nations heritage - his maternal grandfather, Bill Irving, being part of the Stolen Generations.

Northern Territory

In the Northern Territory gold was discovered in 1870. The long and continuous history of gold mining there took place on three main goldfields - Pine Creek, Tennant Creek and the Tanami.

Given the isolation of working in the Northern Territory and the harsh conditions on the goldfields, it was thought that few European would be willing to try making their fortune on the goldfields.

The Chinese arrived in the Northern Territory in 1874 having been recruited by the South Australian government that controlled the Territory at the time to work on the goldfields. Nearly 200 Chinese were brought from Singapore to work in the Territory.

Later they worked building the railway from Darwin to Pine Creek.

The Chinese labour force had to work there for two years in exchange for wages and fares to Australia. Once their term was up most Chinese stayed on to work independently as prospectors.

More Chinese came. By 1885 a large component of the population in the Northern Territory was Chinese. In 1888 there were more than 7,000 Chinese people living in the Territory outnumbering the Europeans.

Even though the Chinese never experienced the same degree of anti-Chinese sentiment as occurred in NSW and Victoria the government in 1888 introduced a £10 tax on Chinese entering the Northern Territory.

As a result, fewer Chinese wanted to work there. A lot of Chinese had already left the Northern Territory and returned to China. A thousand remained in the Territory and by the end of the century, most of them had moved to Darwin[43].

The Chinese that remained worked their own claims, set up market gardens and were involved in industry and commerce, not only on the goldfields. The Chinese were the backbone of the transport and building industries.

Successful Chinese businessman

A successful business entrepreneur in the Northern Territory was Kwong Sue Duk. As a teenager, he went to California where he got his first bucket of gold.

In 1874, Kwong Sue Duk returned to China and studied herbal medicine. One year later (1875), he came to Cooktown and set up a

---

[43] Webber, Kimberley (2012) *Growing Up on the Goldfields*. South Yarra, Vic., Macmillan Education. p. 27

business selling tools and supplies to Chinese gold miners.

In 1879, when the gold rush in Palmer declined he went back to China but he returned again to Australia in 1882.

This time, he set up a business called 'Sun Mow Loon' in Southport in the Northern Territory, situated near Darwin. He sold general goods and real estate.

With the booming Chinese population in Southport and surrounding goldfields, Kwong's business made him a millionaire with a turnover in trade at the time of £25,000 per year [44].

The Chine contributed greatly to the early development of the Northern Territory. Not just miners or rail coolies they worked as carpenters, bricklayers, stonemasons, cabinet-makers, boiler makers and fitters in the local construction industry.

---

[44] Rutian, Mi (2020) "Chinese Business History in Queensland - Gold rush: 1851-1881" State Library of Queensland https://www.slq.qld.gov.au/blog/chinese-business-history-queensland-gold-rush-1851-1881)

Some Chinese played a significant role in private enterprise in pre-war Darwin. Up to 1942, most of the stores around Cavenagh Street were owned by the Chinese [45].

Western Australia

In Western Australia, the first Chinese immigrant was Moon Chow. He arrived in the West either in 1828 or 1829.

Legend has it that Moon Chow was rescued following a shipwreck or he arrived in Albany aboard some form of transport carrying horses.

There are various stories about how he arrived in Western Australia and over time the legend has changed and the story developed.

He worked as a boat builder and carpenter. Eventually, he married an English woman by the name of Mary Thorpe in 1847. They had three children. Moon Chow died in 1877

---

[45] Mo Yimei (1988) *Harvest of Endurance: a History of the Chinese in Australia 1788-1988* Sydney, Australia-China Friendship Society. http://www.multiculturalaustralia.edu.au/doc/yimei_1.pdf

following an accident involving a horse and a cart[46].

In 1847 because of the shortage of a labour force, some 20 Chinese were brought to Western Australia from Singapore. More came in the following year.

The Western Australian colony actively supported the immigration scheme and Singapore became the main source of cheap Chinese labour.

Just like in the eastern states Chinese immigrants were male. Some married European women; and others, although discouraged by the colonial authorities, cohabited with First Nations women.

The life of Chinese men was a lonely one so they fell into gambling, visiting prostitutes and smoking opium.

When gold was discovered in Western Australia tensions between Europeans and

---

[46] http://www.wanowandthen.com/Chinese-in-Western-Australia.html

Chinese surfaced. The Chinese began competing for mining space on the goldfields.

Gold was publicly discovered in 1893 and the discoveries in the west triggered the last of the great Australian gold rushes.

As news about the new discovery spread, hundreds of diggers descended onto the field pegging out new claims at Kalgoorlie and then elsewhere in the region. Kalgoorlie became a mecca for thousands who had suffered the effects of the 1890s depression.

By 1901 many Chinese lived in the Perth and Fremantle areas.

Initially, there was little opposition to the Chinese who worked in the northwest in places that were unattractive to European workers.

But when the contracts for Chinese workers started to expire the Chinese moved south. This was when the Chinese started competing with the Europeans and tensions festered.

By 1893 the immigration scheme wound down but this did not deter Chinese immigration.

Compared to the East, though, the numbers of Chinese in the West were small reaching around 2,000 in 1897.

When Chinese immigration was severely restricted in the East, Western Australia was seen as an alternative avenue for entering the country.

Once the gold rushes were over, those who did not return to China stayed on in Australia finding work as market gardeners and supplying their region with fresh fruit and vegetables.

The Chinese that stayed in Australia made valuable contributions to society in all the Australian colonies. They became prominent in economic development, the restaurant business, small business, horticulture, in medicine, accountancy, public administration and architecture.

Mei Quong Tart

One of the celebrated Chinese entrepreneurs and personalities of the late 1800s was Mei Quong Tart (1850-1903).

Born in Guangdong he was one of the most important business leaders of the Chinese community in Australia [47].

At the young age of nine, he persuaded his uncle to take him to Australia who was taking a shipload of Chinese workers there.

Mei Quong Tart learned English and he went to live with the family of Percy Simpson who treated him like a son. Percy Simpson had leased a large paddock known as Bell's Creek on the Braidwood goldfields. His claims were worked by hundreds of miners most of whom were Chinese.

By the age of eighteen Mei Quong Tart had become wealthy as he had acquired shares in an important claim. He was soon employing Chinese and Europeans on his claim.

Mei Quong Tart became very much part of the life on the goldfields. In Braidwood and Araluen he was prominent in sporting,

---

[47] Lea-Scarlett, E. J. "Mei Quong Tart (1850–1903)", *Australian Dictionary of Biography*, National Centre of Biography, Australian National University, https://adb.anu.edu.au/biography/mei-quong-tart-4181/text6719)

cultural, and religious affairs and was a patron of the local cricket team and local horse races.

In 1881 Quong visited his family in China. When he returned to Australia he opened a tea and silk store in Sydney and became a successful tea and silk merchant.

In 1886 he married an English woman, Margaret Scarlett.

Mei Quong Tart was active in the campaign for the suppression of opium imports and in 1883 he was involved in an investigation of the Chinese camps in southern New South Wales.

In 1888 he was appointed a mandarin of the fifth degree by the Chinese Emperor and he again visited China. On his third Chinese tour in 1894, he was advanced in rank to a mandarin of the fourth degree.

In Sydney, Quong continued his work as a businessman. In 1889 he opened an elaborate restaurant in King Street in Sydney's CBD. Some years later he had a dining hall in the new Queen Victoria Markets.

In 1902 there was an attempt on his life and within a year he was dead.

Mei Quong Tart's funeral was widely covered in the newspapers. Two hundred men escorted his coffin to the Rookwood Cemetery in Sydney, his body dressed in the ceremonial robes of a Mandarin,.

Mei Quong Tart's life had been one of outstanding success not only in business but in community service.

In Summary

The Chinese displayed immense courage in coming to Australia. Driven by hope, they left their villages in Southern China and journeyed to a foreign and hostile country.

They had to meet challenges such as having to journey hundreds of kilometres on foot from Robe in South Australia to the goldfields in Victoria.

The Chinese were abused, they were misunderstood and they encountered discrimination. They were hated by the Europeans just because they were different. The riots in the Buckland Valley and at Lambing Flat demonstrated the depth of that hatred.

Anti-Chinese attitudes and the fear of competition on the goldfields resulted in discriminatory legislation - the 1855 Act and future legislation can only be described as institutionalised racism.

This anti-Chinese sentiment spread from state to state, and, by 1901, the nation adopted its White Australia Policy.

Hopeful immigrants were forced to take a dictation test in any European language. Most Chinese had little education so there was little chance of success.

Those who were already in Australia and who passed the test were subject to discrimination and had their economic activities restricted. Other Chinese migrants who failed the test and who had no passage back to China, fell into depression and despair[48].

Many Chinese that remained in Australia went on to contribute greatly to this country.

The year 1973 was a milestone in the history of the Chinese in Australia. The White Australia Policy was abolished by the Whitlam Government. Al Grassby, a high-profile Minister for Immigration in the Whitlam

---

[48] Mo Yimei, *ibid*, p.7

government, was best known for his role in the initiation of multiculturalism and the ending of the White Australia Policy.

And now...

In the next and fourth book in this series, *Ghosts of Gold: The Life and Times of Jupiter Mosman* learn about the First Nations boy who discovered gold at Charters Towers in 1871.

The Charters Towers goldfield is Australia s largest high-grade gold deposit. Historically it was Australia s largest high-grade gold producer of 6,600,000 ounces of gold ore averaging 38g/t.

The gold discovered by Jupiter Mosman was very profitable and in today s dollars, an estimated one billion dollars in dividends were paid out to its shareholders.

The quality of the gold ore grade from the Charters Towers mines was estimated to be almost double that of the Victorian goldfields and almost 75 per cent higher than grades of

Western Australian (Kalgoorlie) goldfields at that time [49].

---

[49] Citigold Corporation https://www.citigold.com/

Sources

The author would like to acknowledge the following sources of information:

"A history of the Department of Immigration: managing migration to Australia." (2018) Australian Broadcasting Commission https://www.abc.net.au/news/2018-06-10/first-chinese-settlers-descendants-reconnect-with-their-roots/9845804

Aitchison, James (2019) "Non-fiction: madness and massacre: Chinese miners on the Victorian Goldfields" Storgy Magazine in Arts & Culture, Non-Fiction, January. https://storgy.com/2019/01/17/non-fiction-madness-and-massacre-chinese-miners-on-the-victorian-goldfields-by-james-aitchison/

Britannica "Lambing Flat Riots" https://www.britannica.com/event/Lambing-Flat-Riots)

Brown, Cash "The treks from Robe" https://victoriancollections.net.au/media/exhibitions/5fbd874fd5fa8108043fc293//5fc8d9e89992142684f04d6a/original.pdf

Burke, Heather & Grimwade, Gordon (2013) *The Historical Archaeology of the Chinese in Far North Queensland* Vol. 16 https://www.academia.edu/7250100/Historical_Archaeology_of_the_Chinese_in_far_north_Queensland

CBHS Year 5 History http://cbhsyearfivehistory.weebly.com/chinese-miner-riots.html

Citigold Corporation https://www.citigold.com/

Department of Home Affairs (2018) "China-born Community Information Summary" https://www.homeaffairs.gov.au/mca/files/2016-cis-china.pdf

Eureka Centre Ballarat (2022) "Ballarat Harmony Fest - the Chinese Miners' 'Residence Tax Revolt' of 1859" https://www.eurekacentreballarat.com.au/ballarat-harmony-fest-chinese-miners-residence-tax-revolt-1859

Fung, Pamie (2015) "The significance of the first anti-Chinese legislation in Australia" https://peril.com.au/topics/politics/anti-chinese-legislation-in-australia/

Grassby, Al & Hill, Marji (2000) *Chinese Australians.* South Yarra, Vic, Macmillan.

Guoth, Nicholas & Macgregor, Paul (2019) "Getting Chinese Gold off the Victorian Goldfields" *Chinese Southern Diaspora Studies*, 8.

Harris, Lauren Carroll (2018) "The riots history erased: reckoning with the racism of Lambing Flat" The Guardian, 7 August https://www.theguardian.com/artanddesign/2018/aug/07/the-riots-history-erased-reckoning-with-the-racism-of-lambing-flat

Hill, Marji (2021) *Australian Aboriginal History: 5 Stories of Indigenous Heroes*. Gold Coast, Qld, The Prison Tree Press.

Jack, Ian; Holmes, Kate, and Kerr, Ruth (1984) "Ah Toy's Garden: A Chinese Market-Garden on the Palmer River Goldfield, North Queensland" *Australian Historical Archaeology*, 2: 52 (http://www.asha.org.au/pdf/australasian_historical_archaeology/02_04_Jack.pdf)

Lea-Scarlett, E. J. "Mei Quong Tart (1850–1903)", *Australian Dictionary of Biography*, National Centre of Biography, Australian National University, https://adb.anu.edu.au/biography/mei-quong-tart-4181/text6719)

Lote Agency (2021) "A Brief History of Chinese Migration to Australia" https://www.loteagency.com.au/a-brief-history-of-chinese-migration-to-australia/

McGowan, Barry "The Braidwood district's Chinese heritage" Braidwood & District Historical Society. http://braidwoodmuseum.org.au/Chinese.html

Mo Yimei (1988) *Harvest of Endurance: a History of the Chinese in Australia 1788-1988* Sydney, Australia-China Friendship Society. http://www.multiculturalaustralia.edu.au/doc/yimei_1.pdf

Monument Australia https://monumentaustralia.org.au/themes/government/dissent/display/30547-buckland-riot

Mulvaney, D. J. (1969) *The Prehistory of Australia.* London, Thames & Hudson.

National Museum Australia https://www.nma.gov.au/explore/features/harvest-of-endurance/scroll/early-chinese-migrants#:~:text=The%20earliest%20known%20Chinese%20immigrant,and%20purchased%20land%20at%20Parramatta.

National Museum of Australia "Chinese gold miners" https://www.nma.gov.au/explore/features/harvest-of-endurance/scroll/chinese-gold-miners#:~:text=There%20were%20over%2011%2C000%20Chinese,%2C%20Tambaroora%2C%20Tamworth%20and%20Tumut.

Robb, Sandi (2019) *North Queensland's Chinese Family Landscape: 1860-1920.* PhD Thesis

Rutian, Mi (2020) "Chinese Business History in Queensland - Gold rush: 1851-1881" State Library of Queensland https://www.slq.qld.gov.au/blog/chinese-business-history-queensland-gold-rush-1851-1881

Thompson, S. (2011) "1860 Lambing Flat *Roll Up* Banner" Sydney, Migration Heritage Centre, Power House Museum. https://www.migrationheritage.nsw.gov.au/exhibition/objectsthroughtime/lambingflatsbanner/index.html

Victorian Collections https://victoriancollections.net.au/stories/many-roads-stories-of-the-chinese-on-the-goldfields

Washington, Edward "Chinese on the Goldfields" Sydney Living Museums https://sydneylivingmuseums.com.au/stories/chinese-goldfields#:~:text=In%201901%20the%20now%20federal,to%20be%20allowed%20to%20enter.

Webber, Kimberley (2012) *Growing Up on the Goldfields*. South Yarra, Vic., Macmillan Education.

Western Australia Now and Then http://www.wanowandthen.com/Chinese-in-Western-Australia.html

Wright, Tony (2020) "A thorny trail from Buckland to our battles with Beijing" *The Age*, December 5

Yang, Eugene (2018) "Chinese and Indigenous Australians share a long, 'untold history' that's been captured through art" https://www.abc.net.au/news/2018-06-23/indigenous-and-chinese-relationship-in-australian-history/9893920

Questions for further Consideration

What challenges did the Chinese face when they migrated to Australia in the nineteenth century?

How have the Chinese influenced Australian society today?

What is the current relationship between Australia and China?

Gold! Hidden Stories of Australia's Past,
Book 3

About Marji Hill

Artist & Author

Marji Hill, artist and painter since childhood, runs her art career alongside her career as an author.

Marji is a highly respected international author as well as a seasoned business executive, researcher and coach.

She is passionate about promoting understanding between Australia's first people and other Australians.

Marji has fostered the spirit of reconciliation in all her writings since she was Research Fellow in Education at the Australian Institute of Aboriginal and Torres Strait Islander Studies (AIATSIS) in Canberra.

From 2008 to 2011, Marji was Deputy Chairperson of the Mosman Branch of Reconciliation Australia in Sydney.

Following her Education Research Fellowship at AIATSIS in 1976 Marji, together with her late partner, Alex Barlow, produced more than seventy (70) books on all aspects of the First Nations people including the critical, annotated bibliography *Black Australia*.

In 1989 Marji was the Project Coordinator and one of the researchers and writers of *Australian Aboriginal Culture* the official Australian Government publication on First Nations people..

In 1988 her work of non-fiction *Six Australian Battlefields*, which she co-authored with Al Grassby, was published by Angus and Robertson. A decade later it was re-published by Allen & Unwin as a paperback edition.

Her nine-volume encyclopaedia, *Macmillan Encyclopaedia of Australia's Aboriginal*

Peoples was published in 2000 and in 2009 she published *The Apology: Saying Sorry To The Stolen Generations.*

Marji's more recent publications extend to self-improvement and self-help with books like *Staying Young Growing Old* and *Inspired by Country* a self-help book about painting with gouache.

Marji artworks range from very large oil paintings on canvas (her largest being 213 x 167cm) to very small works on paper - gouache being a favourite medium.

Black/white relations, reconciliation, Eureka, and the discovery of gold are common themes not only in her writings but also in her art.

Her small paintings are simple responses to land and sea environments.

Painting has been a lifetime passion for Marji. She remembers as a child winning first prize for a painting she exhibited at the Southport agricultural show. Then in her teens for two years in a row, she won the Sunday Mail Child Art Competition in Queensland with her winning paintings getting full coverage in colour in the newspaper.

Marji's formal art training took place in the 1980s at the Canberra School of Art which in 1992 became ANU School of Art & Design.

As soon as she completed her Master of Arts Degree in Anthropology at the Australian National University (ANU), Marji went on to get a Post Graduate Diploma in Painting. She has held eight solo exhibitions in Canberra, Melbourne and Sydney and she has participated in various group shows.

One of her large paintings was included in the 2004-2005 Art Gallery of Ballarat Traveling Exhibition *Eureka Revisited: the Contest of Memories*. This exhibition travelled to Melbourne, Canberra and Ballarat - part of the 150-year celebration of the Eureka Stockade.

Two of her large paintings were commissioned by the Citigold Corporation. One hang for many years in the foyer of Jupiter's Casino in Townsville until the casino was sold, becoming The Ville Resort-Casino.

Jupiter's Lucky Strike celebrates the discovery of gold by First Nations boy, Jupiter Mosman in 1871 at Charters Towers in North Queensland. This painting today hangs in the offices of the Citigold Corporation in Charters Towers.

The other, a portrait of Jupiter Mosman resides in the World Centre in Charters Towers.

Marji's paintings are in many private collections both in Australia and overseas and she is represented in the Art Gallery of Ballarat and the Ballarat and Sydney campuses of the Australian Catholic University.

For many years Marji travelled extensively both within Australia and internationally, working as a consultant, doing speaking engagements, motivating people, and developing her art career.

Marji has returned to her birthplace and now resides in Surfers Paradise. She

pursues her interests of writing, painting, mentoring, publishing, and internet marketing.

Gold! Hidden Stories of Australia's Past,
Book 3

More Books by Marji Hill

Self-improvement/Self-Help

Hill, Marji 2014 *Staying Young Growing Old.* Broadbeach, Qld, The Prison Tree Press.

Hill, Marji 2020 *How Big Is Your Why? An Author's Guide to Time Management and Productivity to Achieve Transformational Results.* Broadbeach, Qld, The Prison Tree Press.

Hill, Marji 2020 *A Create and Publish Toolbox: 101 Prompts In A Guided Journal To Help You Write, Self publish, And Market Your Book On Amazon.* Broadbeach, Qld, The Prison Tree Press.

Hill, Marji 2021 *Inspired by Country: an Artist's Journey Back to Nature, Landscape Painting with Gouache.* Broadbeach, Qld, The Prison Tree Press.

Gold! Hidden Stories of Australia's Past, Book 3

First Nations

Hill, Marji 2021 *First People Then And Now: Introducing Indigenous Australians.* 2nd ed. Broadbeach, Qld, The Prison Tree Press.

Hill, Marji 2021 *Australian Aboriginal History: 5 Stories of Indigenous Heroes.* Broadbeach, Qld, The Prison Tree Press.

Gold

Hill, Marji (2022) *Gates of Gold: The Discovery of Gold, its Legacy and its Contribution to Australian Identity* Broadbeach, Qld, The Prison Tree Press.

Hill, Marji (2022) *Shadows of Gold: Eureka and the Birth of Australian Democracy.* Broadbeach, Qld, The Prison Tree Press.

Hill, Marji (2022) *Gold and the Chinese: Racism, Riots and Protest on the Australian Goldfields.* Broadbeach, Qld, The Prison Tree Press.

Hill, Marji (2022) *Ghosts of Gold: The Life and Times of Jupiter Mosman.* Broadbeach, Qld, The Prison Tree Press.

Hill, Marji (2022) *Blood Gold: Native Police, Bushrangers & Lawlessness on the Australian Goldfields.* Broadbeach, Qld, The Prison Tree Press.

www.ingramcontent.com/pod-product-compliance
Lightning Source LLC
Chambersburg PA
CBHW041459010526
44107CB00044B/1508